# THE 100 BEST
# CONTEMPORARY INTERIORS

BETA-PLUS

# THE 100 BEST
## CONTEMPORARY INTERIORS

# CONTENTS

# MINIMALIST CHIC

Architect Pascal van der Kelen was commissioned to fit out the
reception rooms in this house to the south of Brussels.

www.pascalvanderkelen.com

All of the walls were painted and museum lighting was installed.

↖
On the ground floor, natural stone flooring was laid throughout all of the rooms.

# DARK/LIGHT CONTRASTS

This house, created by architect Pascal van der Kelen, consists of a
U-shaped ground floor with an inner courtyard that brings
the evening sun into the living area. The L-shaped upper floor is smaller.
The living room looks out onto the inner courtyard and the garden behind. Dark/
light contrasts both outside and inside: dark polyurethane floors and white walls.

www.pascalvanderkelen.com

The kitchen-cum-dining area is in white lacquer work and dark-tinted wood. White resin work surface.

## STARK SYMMETRY

The starkly symmetrical structure of this house is emphasised by the centrally positioned exterior staircase leading from street level to the main storey, which is on the same level as the back garden. The use of glass for the exterior walls demonstrates that they do not have a load-bearing function; they merely enclose the space and reflect the green surroundings. This transparency makes it appear as though the partially covered front and back terraces are inside the building. This is even more apparent when seen from inside: columns and beams support the roof and canopies that extend outside, all of which are made from exposed concrete. A system of partitions has been installed in the open space. Some of the walls reach the ceiling, whilst others allow light to flow over the ceiling.

www.pascalvanderkelen.com

From the entrance hall you can see right through to the back garden. A partition wall, which stops just short of the concrete ceiling, screens off the dining room from the hall.

↖
The living room with a view through to the entrance. In the foreground to the left is the concrete suspended wall containing the smoke shaft for the fireplace. This wall, together with the unit below, reinforces the horizontal character of the living room.

# A RENOVATED HOLIDAY HOME
## BESIDE THE BAY OF SAINT-TROPEZ

This villa beside the bay of Saint-Tropez was designed in 1950 by architect Raymond Louis, who was also a leading designer; his creations included the Coca Cola bottle and the Shell logo. In recent years, this beautifully situated holiday home has been renovated and extended by Belgian architect Michel Lesot from Arquennes. Gilles de Meulemeester (Ebony Interiors) was responsible for the interior design; the kitchen is a creation by Zen Design from Saint-Tropez.

www.ebony-interiors.com

A beige natural stone, Antalya cream, has been used for the living areas. Red combined with beige is the main colour scheme throughout the property.

The Moroccan vases were supplied by Ebony.

↖
The sofas with their white cotton covers are by Tacchini. All of the throws and cushions were supplied by Ebony, as were the coffee table (Artelano) and the standing lamps (by Modénature).

# A MODERN RESIDENTIAL BLOCK
# WITH A BREATHTAKING SEA VIEW

Collection Privée is a renowned interior-design store with branches in Cannes and Valbonne. The company also has a studio for architecture and interior design, headed by Gilles Pellerin and Nicolette Schouten. The project in this report is the architectural studio's most recent creation on the Côte d'Azur: a defiantly contemporary variant on the Provençal villa. Geometric shapes, symmetry and balance are the key to this simply designed block.

www.collection-privee.com

The kitchen work
surface is in Corian.
Custom-built oak
kitchen units.

↖
The entrance door is in zinc.

15

Sofas and coffee tables
are by Baltus (Collection
Privée). A Flexform
armchair.

# CREATIVITY AS A DRIVING FORCE

Wilfra ID&E is a team of enthusiastic furniture makers and interior architects who have mastered the art of introducing a personal and timeless touch into every living and working space. The company was founded in 1953 and initially manufactured only kitchens, but their activities have expanded to include complete interior-design projects at home and abroad. Wilfra ID&E is all about creativity, anticipating market trends and finding inventive solutions.

www.wilfra.be

This kitchen was installed in a new-build home in Uccle, in collaboration with Brussels-based interior-design studio Ensemble & Associés.
A streamlined interplay of colours: white Silestone combined with black oak veneer.
To ensure a calm and serene atmosphere, Silestone was the only variety of stone used throughout this kitchen: for the floors, surfaces, walls and shelves.

# A SOPHISTICATED FINISH FOR A 400 M² LOFT

This loft is in an industrial building that was completely transformed by architectural studio Edena, who created rock gardens in this residential island and converted the building into lofts. For the design of the ground-floor area, a former printing business of 400 m², the new owners brought in the services of interior architect Anne Derasse. The site had no interesting industrial structures: as a contrast with the lofts, which were left in an original and basic state, the challenge for Derasse consisted of providing a sophisticated finish for this home, right down to the smallest details.

www.annederasse.be

The long fireplace is an eye-catching feature that incorporates the only slanting wall in the loft and also the multimedia unit. Minotti sofas, PK 22 armchairs designed by Poul Kjaerholm and a B.I.C. carpet.

Table in rustic oak by S. Lebrun. Casamilano chairs with fabric covers. The green pouf is by B&B Italia.

↖
The furniture was chosen for its timelessly sober appeal and streamlined design, softened here and there by a more relaxed element, such as the chaise longue. Derasse considered the proportions of this huge space and introduced a number of "over-sized" pieces.
The chaise longue by Paola Lenti has green felt upholstery. Anne Derasse designed the low shelving.

# CONTRAST

Architect Pascal Van der Kelen has completely rebuilt this house. All that remains of the original property is the main building. Van der Kelen removed the entire adjoining pseudo-Tuscan section to make way for a new ground-floor house. The theme of "contrast" was central to the rebuilding and design process, both in the dimensions of the property and in the use of colour. With the clear symmetry of the main building as a starting point, Van der Kelen constructed a new contemporary section, into which he extended the central axis. This sense of unity is further reinforced by the freestanding sections of wall with symmetrical circulation zones to the left and right, and by the two high, open spaces to the left and right of the entrance and the strong symmetry in the arrangement of the seating furniture.

www.pascalvanderkelen.com

# A VERY SYMMETRICAL HOME

At the express request of his client, architect Pascal Van der Kelen designed a very symmetrical home. This symmetry is emphasised by the tall front door. There are three symmetrical windows on the first floor at the front and back of the house: in the centre of the house is the high open space of the hallway, with bedrooms on the right and left. This division into three can also be seen at the rear of the building, both on the ground floor and upstairs. Large sections of enamelled glass alternate with plastered areas and windows. Building regulations required a gable roof: this was kept as subtle as possible and given a zinc finish.

www.pascalvanderkelen.com

Diagonal views of the living room and dining room.

The kitchen was also created to a design by the architect.

↖
From the moment you enter the building, you have a complete view of the living space and the garden behind the house. The entrance hall and the living room can be closed off with sliding panels.

# BAUHAUS INSPIRATION

This home in the German speaking part of Belgium was designed in 2007 by the architect Josef Kirschvink, who was inspired by Bauhaus. Yvonne Hennes (Project by PHYL) realised the total layout of this striking country estate with approximately 360 m² of living space. The challenge consisted of creating both an ideal living environment and a workplace: both functions had to be combined harmoniously and still be kept separate. The left wing of the residence consists of the garage, carport and the living area. The offices of the interior architecture firm are to the right. These two wings are separated by a piece of "sliding furniture": a sliding bookcase adjoining the offices.

www.projectbyphyl.com

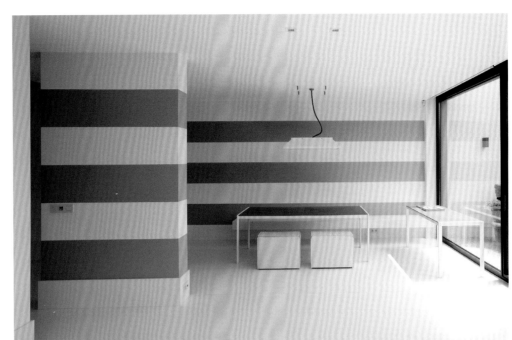

Benches by Piet Boon (Sjoerd) around a San Marco table from Zanotta. Hanging light from Modular, "Diablo".

A table designed and custom made by Yvonne Hennes with "Siebe" chairs by Piet Boon.

# A PERIPHERAL CIRCULATION

The interior walls of this apartment have been designed in such a way as to create a peripheral circulation around the glass walls of the exterior. They provide all of the rooms with a calming view of the North Sea and the beach. The floor throughout has been laid with small glass-mosaic tiles in a dark sand colour. This creates a feeling of texture and is a reference to the grainy effect of the sandy beach, in contrast to the stark white plastering of the walls.

www.pascalvanderkelen.com

The sliding glass screens can be opened separately and provide a view of the sea and the living area.

# A SEASIDE VILLA IN SAINT-TROPEZ

This house "with its feet in the water" in the parkland of Saint-Tropez boasts magnificent views, but had been neglected for many years. Esther Gutmer created a completely new structure, dividing the house into three living spaces, with all rooms enjoying a sea view. The outside areas and the garden were redesigned and offer a splendid 180° panorama. The absence of a parapet ensures an uninterrupted vista. Shades of white, with just a few colourful accents as contrast, were selected for the interior, underlining the character of this haven of beauty.

www.esthergutmer.be

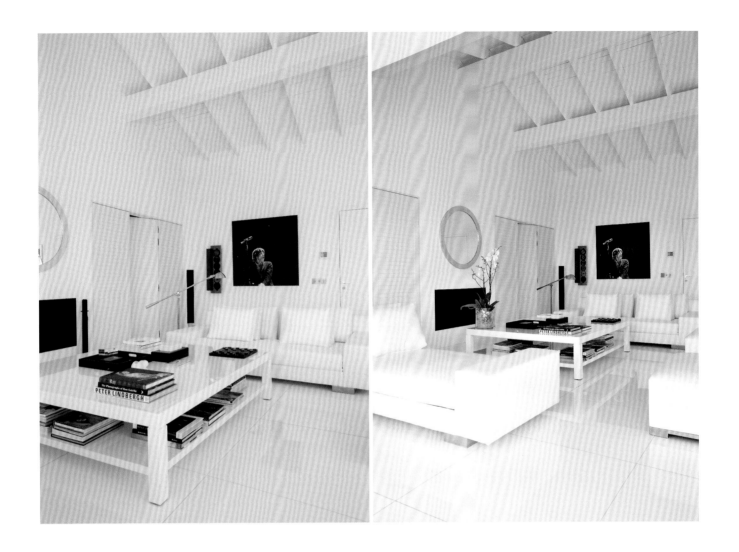

The original roof, with its gentle slope, has been rebuilt.
The visible framework of the building creates a sense of space.

The sitting room, with louvre doors fully integrated into the walls, is completely in white, so as to accentuate the endless blue outside.

# A HOUSE IN UCCLE

The site of this house in Uccle (Brussels) is on a variety of different levels. The main entrance and the garages are at street level. The living areas are situated on the ground floor, on the same level as the garden, and are reached by a staircase that begins in the hallway. The owners are passionate about photographic art, and they asked Esther Gutmer to create an interior that would show their collection to its best advantage.

www.esthergutmer.be

Access to the ground-floor garden level via a staircase in white concrete with a glass banister.

The dining room is an integral part of the living room.
The two spaces are simply separated by a wall panel that conceals the stairs.

↖
The use of white concrete for the floor increases the sense of light in the sitting room. Table and crocodile-skin ottomans designed by Esther Gutmer.

# MAGNIFICENT VIEWS

This metropolitan duplex apartment offers magnificent views and optimum incidence of light. To create a feeling of intimacy, the larger rooms were divided into different areas while retaining the loft concept by not using fixed walls. Although Nathalie Van Reeth selected different materials, she used the same tonality to preserve the loft's atmosphere so that the different areas blend together; a whole picture that radiates peace and serenity.

nathalie.vanreeth@skynet.be

A sitting corner with PK22 white leather chairs by Poul Kjaerholm and a vintage table.

↖
The spectacular staircase is also one of Nathalie Van Reeth's creations.

Behind the sliding wall
with fireplace there
is space for a TV and
sound system.
Vintage furniture and a
vintage Iranian carpet.

# A THOROUGH METAMORPHOSIS

A classical residence underwent a thorough metamorphosis, spurred on by Nathalie Van Reeth. The house was fully stripped, down to the basic structure. The rear was torn open to strengthen the contact with the sunny garden and improve the incidence of light. Materials and colour were added subtly to accentuate the serene atmosphere.

nathalie.vanreeth@skynet.be

The salon looks out over a water feature. Seats and tables according to designs by Nathalie Van Reeth. The chauffeuses are by Christian Liaigre. An antique Afghan carpet and a vintage chair.

Salon and dining room gently flow over into each other, the linear table and the fireplace connect both areas. Two black leather PK22 seats by Poul Kjaerholm.

↖
The fireplace with a large sliding panel behind it for TV and music. The entirety radiates peace through the subtle use of colours.

# A REMARKABLE POOLHOUSE

An extension in wood was added to an existing shower building next to an outdoor swimming pool. This construction's area of attention was creating a new sitting corner with adjoining kitchen and fitness area that was close to the pool and had an open view of the garden. The new areas create a situation where the residents spend many a pleasant occasion with family or friends by the pool, in the midst of nature.

nathalie.vanreeth@skynet.be

Playful combination of mink coloured butterfly chairs (Arne Jacobsen) around a solid oak table.

The open kitchen, with custom varnished mdf cupboards, a cooker-hood finished with a bronze coloured glass mirror and a marble worktop.

↖
The open living area with fireplace, a perfect setting to set up a movie show.
A seat by Flexform and the legendary lounge chair with ottoman by the designer couple Charles and Ray Eames, shown here with a white leather finish.
Floor in grained brown marble tiles.

# A FLOWING CIRCULATION

When this project was entrusted to Ensemble & Associés, the property developer had just taken possession of two separate structurally finished apartments with a total surface area of 350 m². The mission was to create a single duplex with a large reception area and a flowing circulation between the spaces, all in grey-black-white shades.

www.ensembleetassocies.be

All the joinery is finished in
sandblasted and stained larch.

↖
A GroundPiece sofa from
Flexform and a Limited
Edition carpet.

# SURPRISINGLY SPACIOUS

Bart Van Boom (Kultuz) realised the complete metamorphosis of an existing home. The entire living area, from cellar to attic, was revised and suddenly became "surprisingly spacious". The minimalist finish exudes calm, the perspectives have been optimised. The artwork by Maurice Frydman in the living room is the eye catcher. The open fireplace has been integrated in the wall together with a multimedia furniture, architecturally set in the existing walls.

www.kultuz.be

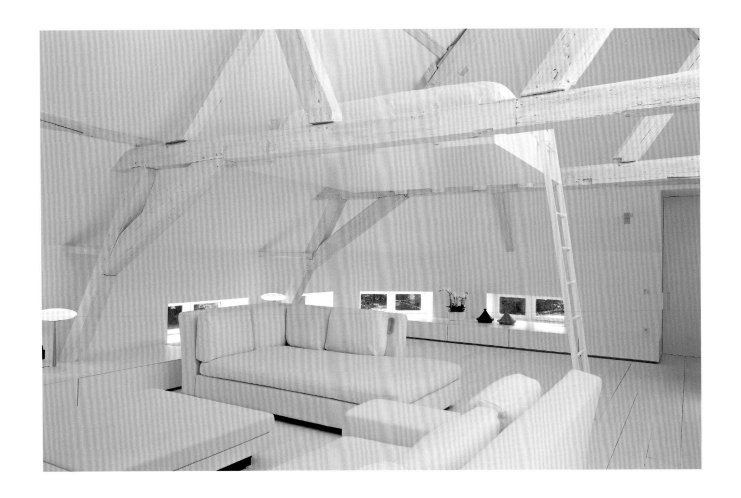

# HARMONY OF WHITE IN AN ANCIENT CASTLE

It took two years for the efforts of Hendrik Vermoortel and Ingrid Lesage to transform Kasteel Ter Heyde in Vladslo (Diksmuide), supposedly founded on a castle-mound structure with origins in the fourteenth century, into a contemporary castle home. Over the course of time, it is intended that this protected monument should develop into a cultural enclave: a meeting place where the arts, as well as philosophy, sociology, architecture and the preservation of historic buildings, can enter into constant interaction.

www.buro2.be

The office with a desk and chair by Ceccotti. The lamp is a design by Philippe Starck for Flos.

## SOPHISTICATED COMBINATION
## OF NATURE AND MODERN ART

This house, built in the 1980s, was designed by architect Marc Corbiau.
The interior was completely redesigned by Obumex a few years ago
to meet the desires of a family with adolescent children.
The result is a building that is both modern and timeless.

www.obumex.be

The choice of furnishings, the colour palette and the discreet, warm lighting were partly inspired by the works of art that were present.

↖
Carpets and curtains have been selected to be in harmony with the floors and furnishings.
Modern art does not only serve as decoration or objet d'art in this house, but forms an essential element of the interior.

## SOBER WHITE AND DARK SHADES
## IN A MODERN DUPLEX APARTMENT

Stephanie Laporte from The Office Belgium designed the interior of this contemporary duplex apartment in West Flanders. The clients, a young couple, wanted a simple, contemporary interior with warm tones. As the apartment is completely enclosed and not much light comes in from outside, the home was finished in pale shades throughout, with a few darker accents for features including the wooden floor and the hall cupboard. The decision to use one model of light fitting throughout the whole apartment also creates a peaceful, calming atmosphere. Obumex and Kordekor were commissioned to carry out the project.

www.stephanielaporte.be     www.obumex.be

The kitchen was built by Obumex. Terrazzo surface, combined with dark-tinted laminated wood.

In the bathroom a pale Cotto d'Este floor is combined with dark natural stone and dark-tinted wood.

## A COSY AND SOBER APARTMENT
## IN A 17TH-CENTURY LISTED BUILDING

This magnificent 80m² apartment is the result of a collaboration between two interior architects: designer John-Paul Welton and Brigitte Boiron, who is also a project developer. There is nothing to suggest that a gem of contemporary living lies behind the facade of this listed seventeenth-century building in the historic centre of Geneva with a view of St. Pierre Cathedral: a cosy and yet sober, streamlined apartment. The secret of this exceptional place: the inspired choice of furniture, colours and materials.

www.projectdesign.ch    www.weltondesign.com

The beams in the sitting room have a white gloss finish. "London" armchairs in calfskin, custom-made by Welton Design.
The lamp to the left of the armchairs is by One By One. The white-leather sofa from the Samira collection is a creation by Welton Design, as is the custom-made white lacquered coffee table.

The Arclinea "Ambiance Cuisine" kitchen has a Corian work surface and white Cube poufs by Welton Design. The hanging lamp is a 1969 design by Verner Panton: Spiral Lamp.

↖
A floor in polished concrete and a carpet in pure white Flokati wool. Elitis blinds (No Limit).
The woodwork is by cabinetmaker Luc Obersson.

## A LUMINOUS MINIMALISM

Olivier Michel, the founder and driving force behind Upptown, is one of the most talked-about project developers of recent years. In a very desirable area of Ukkel (Brussels region), he discovered a group of dilapidated warehouses and garages, which he soon transformed into a residential project with four ultramodern lofts. The intention was to sell all four properties, but Michel and his wife were so enthusiastic about this project that they joined together two of the lofts for themselves to create one large property of over 600m², with its own garden, a swimming pool and two patio areas.

A glamorous harmony of silver and white: a padded wall in silver-coloured vinyl, a fireplace from ABC Interieur with a stainless-steel surround, white epoxy floor and sofa.

An extra large sofa by Minotti and a custom-made coffee table in lacquered MDF with a gleaming black insert.

↖
All of the floors (over 600m²) are in epoxy: cast concrete that is then polished and finished with two layers of paint. The black/white contrasts and the expressionist works by Belgian painter Charles Szymkowicz provide a necessary touch of drama.

## A LOVE OF COLOUR

This large apartment is situated on the top floor of a building surrounded by greenery. It has terraces all around, but, paradoxically, it looked gloomy and cramped. The task of the Baudouin Courtens studio involved completely rethinking the layout and design in order to optimise the light entering the apartment and the connections with the space outside. The living area has been completely opened up, the false ceilings have been removed and huge sliding windows have been installed. The windows, fitted flush to the exterior wall, completely dissolve the boundaries between inside and outside. The designers opted for a completely white space that would allow the owner of this home to express her love of colour through her selection of furniture and art.

www.courtens.be

The Obumex kitchen, with a skylight that creates a bright and airy atmosphere, is organised around a central island and opens onto the dining room.

## TIMELESS AND HARMONIOUS

This stately residence in London's Holland Park was built in 1862 by the architects William & Francis Radford. Winny Vangroenweghe, architect with Obumex, created and coordinated the complete renovation and layout of the premises into a timeless and harmonious whole, where the hectic character of the metropolis is quickly forgotten... Obumex has over half a century's experience in the design and production of exclusive, customised interiors. Since several years the Belgian company also uses this unique know-how for the creation of holiday homes.

www.obumex.be

Central, a work by Vik Muniz.
Furniture by Liaigre, ceramic tiles by Royal Mosa.

The dining room is separated from the kitchen by a glass door.
The large artwork above the bench at the dining table is by German photographer, Elger Esser.
The wall units in the dining room and kitchen form a single, continuous whole.

↖
Most furniture is by Christian Liaigre: for the owner of this residence, he is the trendsetter in elegant, contemporary furniture with a timeless feel.
Rooms with Liaigre furniture never age: they are luxurious, serene, refined and comfortable, all at the same time.
The artwork with black frame is by Hiroshi Sugimoto.
Floor tiles Terra XXL by the Dutch manufacturer Royal Mosa.

The kitchen was conceived as an extension of the living area and is an integral part of it.
The high wall units hide all appliances and storage space.

The kitchen was fully designed and created by Obumex.

# A HOME COLLECTION

Pascal van der Kelen has been one of the leading architects and interior designers of his generation for several years. As well as his own customised architecture and interior designs, he has also recently unveiled his own Home Collection. This apartment shows how Pascal van der Kelen combines bespoke work, made using the architect's drawings, with elements from his Home Collection. This collection includes a wide range of light fittings alongside a kitchen, seating furniture, beds and libraries. The most commonly used materials are bog oak, enamelled glass, synthetic panels and leather, painted metal...

www.pascalvanderkelen.com

The large wall in the dining room is made from black lava rock, just like the library.
Table and ceiling lamp from the Home Collection by Pascal van der Kelen: the table frame in polished stainless steel with bog oak surface, the lamp is a hanging structure made from polished stainless steel with a shade made in brown smoked and frosted glass. Bespoke wool carpet.
The view from the sleeping area to the dining room can be screened off thanks to the painted sliding door.

The kitchen from the Home Collection by Pascal van der Kelen, here finished with front lower cupboards in enamelled glass, work surface with synthetic panels, and storage cupboards in bog oak.

↖
Seating furniture by Minotti with the frame in polished stainless steel and covered with grey flannel (for the long bench) and cognac-coloured leather (all single seats).
All frame finishing in wooden strips.

# CARTE BLANCHE

Interior architect Sarah Lavoine was given a carte blanche for this complete project in the heart of Paris: the transformation of a duplex apartment with 250 m² + 200 m² terraces. The renovation works took a long time because the original kitchen and entrance hall were situated on the upper floor. Sarah Lavoine designed these rooms below, so the eighth floor could be devoted completely to the master bedroom with desk, dressing room, bathroom and wet room. The whole thing was completely redesigned by Sarah Lavoine's team: creation of the spaces, customisation, the succession of volumes…

www.sarahlavoine.com

A contemporary living environment in a loft style, with hi-tech gadgets and home automation. The coffee table was found at an antique dealer's. In the background above, the terrace with the black wall panels and bright red terracotta pot by Domani.

↖
A strong feeling of space and transparency in the entrance hall. The oak parquet floor was painted white and contrasted with the black bespoke work. A carpet on the stairs by Hartley. Pouenat wall lamp and "La Chaise" armchair by Eames.

# CASA NERO

Casa Nero refers to the name of the interior design agency of the owners (Casa Vero) and to the black brick volume that makes up their home, designed by BBSC-Architects. Closed on the roadside (strengthened by the patio where the public area switches to the private area) but completely open towards the broad meadow landscape at the back, which makes contact with nature optimal. Open plan inside, a central rigid box in the middle that still provides some division without completely cutting off the contact between the areas. All the utility functions are housed in this volume, cloakroom, toilet, laundry and cool storage. This means the ground floor can be used flexibly; central kitchen, lounge area with connection to the garage, living room, etc. can be used together as larger rooms.

www.casavero.be

## A VERY SPACIOUS FEEL

Due to the old land division the location of the home, designed by the firm of architect Hans Verstuyft, is different to that of the surroundings. The home is situated to the rear of the site, which means that it can be very transparent around and contact with nature is very intensive. The plan consists of loosely placed partitions with a clear structure and a separate experience of space. Different circuits are created that connect the rooms. The interim partitions define the functions in a light way. Each room retains its unique character but the link between the spaces can be felt well. This creates a very spacious feel. This principle is also repeated on the first floor.

www.hansverstuyftarchitecten.be

## LONG VISTAS

This 85-m² loft is defined by two structures: the original concrete structure of the building (the ancient mills of Ruysbroeck) and the new volume where various functions were brought together. The existing brick walls, concrete beams and balcony were retained and painted white to make the space as light as possible, in contrast with the solid character of the building. The new volume in smooth plasterwork is entirely separate on both sides of the brick walls originally painted white. Long vistas are made possible in this way, reaching to the Pajottenland meadows.

www.brunovanbesien.be

## OPTIMISING THE SPACE

The floor plan of this magnificently situated apartment by the coast was adapted by Minus at the client's request to optimise the space within the limited area. The living space, kitchen and storage were designed as a single open space with a view of the dunes through the large glass elements. The wall was split up widthways, which created a utility wall that discretely houses all the functions. With much eye for detail all the "irritating" appliances were built in behind pivoting doors. All the doors to the rooms were also integrated in the walls through which you enter the apartment. The built in furnishings were made in grades of white, strengthened with a number of sand coloured highlights that immediately elicit a holiday feel.

www.minus.be

## STRONG PERSPECTIVES
## AND A GREAT FEELING OF SPACE

This 220 m² family home was designed by the architect Bruno Vanbesien. The original home offered little light, had no contact with the garden, was lacking in comfort and was situated on a bizarre piece of land. The traditional structure was overturned by Bruno Vanbesien, the existing building was dismantled and the extensions were demolished. To create rest and serenity all the surfaces were kept rigid and white, with the cupboards in dark shaded zebrano wood as the major contrast. The volumes were respected insofar as possible, for that reason the cupboards are in the walls and all the technical elements (structure, lighting, ventilation, music and heating) are fully integrated. The rigid lines (both horizontal and vertical) ensure strong perspectives and a great feeling of space.

www.brunovanbesien.be

## A WARM TOUCH

As one of the few modern homes in the surroundings, the atmosphere of the
contemporary architecture continues indoors: large and high rooms with a
lot of light, and the use of sober materials in a tight framework.
Obumex's design still results in an interior with a warm touch, the natural
materials, the shades of grey outside and white inside, the balanced
colour packages, with here and there a contemporary accent.
This is a project that is fully designed, implemented and co-ordinated by Obumex.

www.obumex.be

# THE CREATIVE SCHOOL

Interior Architect Guillaume Da Silva was given carte blanche for this project: the new interpretation and renovation of an old village school. The building, which had been transformed a lot over the years, had lost all its attraction, but the wonderful sizes betrayed a strong residential potential. The interior designer turned the classroom into a salon. The narrow corridor was broken open, the playground placed in a lawn, with a pool. Fascinated by the quality of light inside the building Guillaume Da Silva used this source to create volumes with refined lines. The whole of the premises was tackled in this way. White is the guiding principle, which was used on all carriers. The materials are treated with lime, the oak floors are bleached, the raw concrete gets a bath... The white linen shows the contrast with the custom-built sections in brushed and tinted oak.

www.guillaumedasilva.com

The entrance hall offers a view towards the garden and pool.

View of the office and the mezzanine above the kitchen.

↖
The reading and music room
has a more intimate fireplace
and a panoramic aquarium.

# HIDDEN LOFT

Architect Karla Menten transformed an existing vacant space in a former Belgacom building in Hasselt into a special loft apartment with an architect's office. She sees her loft as a 21st century «living machine» in which living, relaxing and working are united in a single large room.

www.karlamenten.be

Three extra-large volumes, which are placed diagonally opposite each other, are the only "furniture". They provide privacy where needed and conceal everything functional.

# AN ICON OF CONTEMPORARY MINIMALIST AESTHETICS

An architect-designed bungalow from 1959 was spectacularly transformed
into an icon of contemporary minimalist aesthetics and exclusive modern-
day living comfort by Van Aken Architects of Eindhoven.
Zeth Interior design & construction (interior designer Rob Zeelen)
was responsible for the design of this unique home.

www.vanakenarchitecten.nl     www.zeth.nl

A sofa by Flexform and tables by Ivano Redaelli. The large standard lamp is by Cappellini, the object by Fons Schobbers.

Silver chairs (design by Hadi Teherani) around a JAS table by Jerome Abel Sequin (by Marcel van Dijk of Oogenlust). Nur hanging lamps by Artemide, spotlights by Modular (multiple trimless) and again the Living Divani Extra Wall couch.

## A UNIQUE GARDEN

This project by Jan Joris Landscaping, came about together with the client and in close consultation with architect Frank Van Laere and designer / artist Thierry Lejeune: a unique, contemporary garden in a beautiful setting. Two major lines of sight were used for the work inside the house. Along one axis this was reinforced by a long narrow pond (in aluminium and a path with artwork on the other side). Another axis was subtly drawn from the gate, the door to the whole rear.

www.janjoristuinen.be

The whole consists of an open garden, yet each interior room or walking axis has its own atmosphere.

# FUNCTIONAL MINIMALISM

In this project by the Pascal François architectural studio, minimalist
design is combined with a very functional home.
This property has a streamlined appearance and radiates a sense of simplicity
and calm, but this visual harmony conceals the very latest in technology
and the ceiling-height wall units ensure an optimal use of space.

www.pascalfrancois.be

Above the open fireplace, a long strip in black fabric that conceals the music system.

↖
A view from the first-floor entrance hall towards the kitchen. On the right, continuous wall units with integrated lighting above. Behind these units are the cloakroom, storage space and kitchen equipment.

# TRANSPARENCY, OPENNESS AND GEOMETRY

This recent project by Pascal François is a fine example of the virtuosity with which this architectural studio based in Aalst is able to create practical minimalism. The result is an open living area, offering lots of garden views and with skylights and large windows ensuring plenty of light.

www.pascalfrancois.be

The entrance hall (with a frosted glass door leading to the bathrooms) and a detail of the prefab concrete staircase.

The bathroom with a walk-in shower and a concrete vanity unit on two levels: U-shaped and completely open underneath to allow wheelchair access.
The shower is clad throughout with square black Winckelmans tiles.

↖
The sitting room with a concrete desk unit in the background.

# ART AND DESIGN IN A MINIMALIST SETTING

This minimalist house was designed by Alain Demarquette, an architect from northern France, who was commissioned by clients with a passion for contemporary art and design. Senior interior architect Kurt Neirynck from Obumex designed and supervised the home interior. One of the most important sources of inspiration for this house was the Fondation Beyeler in Basel, a Renzo Piano creation. Grey, white and black are the basic colours that recur throughout this project: this virtually monochrome palette ensures a streamlined and simple look throughout.

www.obumex.be

Works of art by artists
including Andy Warhol
and Victor Vasarely in the
open space containing the
sitting room and dining
room. Table by Le Corbusier
and chairs by Knoll.

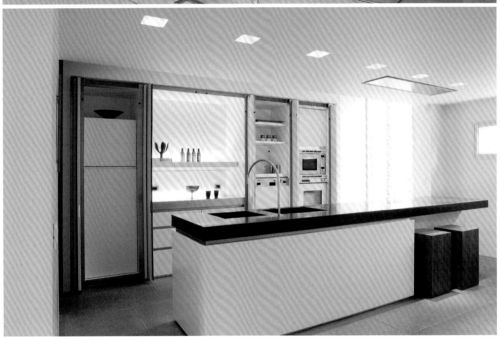

The kitchen was created
by Obumex to a design
by John Pawson.

↖
Design occupies a prominent
position in this house in
northern France.
Concrete tiles were selected
for the floor. The stairs are
also cast in concrete.

# AN ANCHORING POINT

The client bought this apartment in the shell construction phase so that the interior architects
Koen Aerts and Roos Blower could experiment with the position of the non-load-bearing walls.
As a result, they could tailor their design work precisely to meet the client's
requirements, with the focus on relaxation and freedom from stress.
The kitchen has been moved and has become the anchoring point of the living space.

www.aerts-blower.be

To make the most of this space, the wall bench in the dining area has an integrated storage space.

## A ROOF APARTMENT
## WITH A BEAUTIFUL NATURAL VIEW

In a charming town, the team of interior architects Koen Aerts and Roos Blower have designed
a roof apartment in a beautiful natural environment. A conscious effort has been made to
keep the design lines and forms sober and restrained. In contrast, the choice of materials
is lavish and natural: white marble from Carrara, walnut and oak, wool and linen.

www.aerts-blower.be

The night hall is white and sober, with doors integrated in the wall surface and floors made of white Carrara marble.

↖
The family can read or watch TV while relaxing in the lounge chair, a design classic by Eames which is still in continuous production at Vitra.

# SOBER HARMONY IN A CITY APARTMENT

This apartment was purchased by the client as seen. The firm of architects Stein Van Rossem designed the interior according to the client's requirements. The interior designers were commissioned to create an atmosphere that transcends everyday life, exuding austerity and harmony. Based on these requirements, a single unit was crafted by eliminating all possible excrescences and generating a pure, uncluttered design. All potentially disruptive elements are hidden from view, and emphasis is placed on the aesthetic experience: a pleasant feeling of light, perspective and materials within a tight framework that does not give the impression of being excessively sterile.

www.steinvanrossem.be

The tailor-made TV unit and the coffee table, both made of red stained oak veneer, are the focus of all the attention in this "cool white" area. The closed door panels behind the sofa conceal the home office.

Extending out from the home office, the open-plan kitchen consists of a wall element that houses all the kitchen utensils and a freestanding block with a high back that also serves as a visual buffer.

↖
The dining area and lounge form one single unified whole. Because of the shape of the apartment, a round table was selected for the dining area.

# EXTRA LIGHT

This splendid villa was transformed into the offices of Arplus Projects.
Extra light is admitted through the curtain wall over two floors
and everywhere by the use of the white material.
Harmony of white screed, white walls and cupboards to create unity.
Above on this page: a Barcelona chair designed by Mies van der Rohe.

www.arplus.be

The white Bolidt screed was used in all rooms.

This bathroom was designed to be as roomy as possible, with a white screed, Corian bathroom accessories, wide mirrors and a large glass wall.
Design and implementation: AR+.

This kitchen in a modern renovated villa, designed and implemented by AR+, forms the link between the dining areas and the sitting room.
The use of white materials was extended everywhere. A white kitchen unit in composite material, white painted fronts in MDF and a ready-to-lay oak veneer parquet. The lights are by Oty.

# A SPECIAL ATMOSPHERE

The hall is the central link in this house, designed by NU Architectuur (Wim Vos). The stairs are fully finished with Italian stucco in a glass casing, which runs over three levels. The blue light creates a special atmosphere next to the flat cupboard wall of wengé veneer with doors lying inside. Wim Vos accentuates the structure and scale, whereby the relatively large rooms are given their own warm character in a taut idiom.

www.nuarchitectuur.com

This kitchen was designed by Wim Vos (NU Architectuur).

The atmosphere in this wine cellar, created by Wim Vos, is purposely trendy. The wine racks are custom-made.

# CONTEMPORARY LIVING ON THE SCHELDT

A young self-employed couple gave interior architect Bert Van Bogaert
carte blanche to design and create a stylish, strictly minimalist loft
for them with a breathtaking view of the river Scheldt.
The generous budget meant that only high-quality materials were used, and it
was possible to devote attention to the finish of even the smallest details.

bert.vanbogaert@pandora.be      www.interieurdemaere.be

The kitchen was designed and manufactured by Interieur De Maere.

The floating sink area is in basalt. The sunken bath has been clad with the same natural stone. The cupboards above have sliding mirrors.

↖
Above the gas fire, a plasma screen has been built into the wall. The air-conditioning has also been incorporated into the wall and fitted with a subtle vent that runs the length of the fire. The ceiling-height windows provide a perfect view over the Scheldt from the sitting room.

# PLAYING WITH LIGHT AND SPACE

This contemporary house, a compact volume that is entirely focused on the exterior, was created by Baudouin Courtens for an "artist of light". Light is the theme that runs throughout this house: in both its natural and its artificial forms. The choice of materials was driven by an urge to use natural elements and shades: brown terracotta roof tiles, copper guttering and drains, lime plasterwork, bluestone and grey windows.

www.courtens.be

The entrance hall, which forms the distribution axis to the different spaces in this house, is the ideal place to exhibit the owner's art collection. Works by Laurence Demaison and Yves Ullens.

The main bathroom is designed as a contrast of white and dark brown: polished and bushhammered white Carrara marble and tinted oak furniture.

↖
The sitting room forms the heart of the house: it opens onto the garden, the interior spaces (the hall, the music room) and the stairs. A long lava-stone bench provides space for the wrought-iron open fireplace. The music system has been incorporated into the chimney breast. The colour palette consists of muted shades, contrasting sharply with the explosion of colours in the works by Claire Corey, Jean-Luc Moerman and Yves Ullens.

# LIGHT, SPACE, VISION

"Ensemble & Associés": two female interior designers have combined their efforts in this company, following a strict and unique method of working since its inception. They look at the role of light and of details in a new and unusual way, coupling this approach with a thorough knowledge of the client's requirements: every project is carried out in symbiosis with the client's vision. Their hallmark is the idea of complementarity, as is demonstrated by the design of this 300m² home in the heart of the Belgian capital.

www.ensembleetassocies.be

The kitchen was created by Bulthaup.
Floor in Cotto d'Este and a work surface in grey composite stone.

The entrance hall. A specially designed console in tinted oak and bronze.

↖
The parquet floor was made in grey-tinted oak with a matt varnish finish. A gas corner fire, specially designed and built for this space. The low tinted-oak and bronze tables were also custom-built. Minotti armchairs and a Flexform sofa.

# AIMING FOR THE ESSENCE

This house, idyllically situated in one of the green boroughs of Brussels, was designed by architect Jean-Marie Gillet and furnished by interior designer Jacques Van Haren, who describes this project as an "Essential House": a housing unit in which all of the living functions have been reduced to their absolute essence, blending together to form one large space.

www.jacquesvanharen.com

The central piece of furniture is made of ebony. Panama stools designed by Jacques Van Haren. Bateig natural stone on the floor. The cross-shaped design of the posts is a reference to the structural drawings for Mies van der Rohe's pavilion (1939).

The bathroom in glass and natural stone: solid Bateig stone for the units and flint for the walls.
The skylight and windows can be discreetly dimmed.
The windows open electrically and disappear into the walls.

↖
The sunken living room gives a perfect view of the garden. The sofa materials were chosen to harmonise with the stone details.

# A NEW TRANSPARENCY

Architect Baudouin Courtens was asked to redesign the interior of a house in the hills around Liège. He immediately realised that the arrangement of the spaces within the house no longer corresponded to modern-day lifestyle requirements and also prevented the owners from getting full enjoyment from the wonderful garden. He suggested to the clients that the whole of the ground floor should be restructured and he constructed a new extension to house the sitting room.

www.courtens.be

Fine materials (bluestone, oak, lime paints, linen and leather) in a limited range of colours contribute to the harmonious look of this home. Simplicity and serenity were of key importance in the design of the sitting room: a perfect setting for the owner's art collection.

A view showing the rhythm of the sliding doors: kitchen, dining room, wine cellar and reception room all follow on from each other.

# A WARM COLOUR PALETTE IN A BRUSSELS APARTMENT

A young, dynamic couple contacted Ensemble & Associés and asked the company to furnish an apartment they had recently bought in the centre of Brussels: a bare space, 185m² in size. The task consisted of creating a sense of warmth throughout the spacious apartment and providing an inviting and cosy environment in which to receive friends.

www.ensembleetassocies.be

The kitchen (with a view of the terrace) was also designed by Ensemble & Associés and built in painted tongue-and-groove MDF and composite stone. Dornbracht taps, furniture by Luz Interiors, floor in Cotto d'Este.

↖
The shelving unit, specially designed by Ensemble & Associés and built in Beveka walnut wood, provides a central axis through the apartment.

# A VIEW OF THE SEA

The interior design of this seaside apartment with a magnificent sea view
was created by Stefanie Everaert and Caroline Latour (Doorzon).
Obumex's senior interior architect Tom Sileghem took care of
the technical engineering and the site supervision.
The Van den Weghe stone company carried out all of the stonework.

www.doorzon.be     www.vandenweghe.be

The entire floor of this apartment is in Bianco Statuario marble. This ensures a wealth of light throughout the apartment, from front to back.

Curtains separate the bathrooms and bedrooms.

# ENDLESS VIEWS

Nothing remains of the original appearance of these four houses from the 1950s which were combined into a contemporary and luxurious single-family home. The restructuring of its various levels and functionality revolved around a patio which now lets natural light into the heart of the house. With taste and determination, the owner allowed Oliver and Hélène Lempereur to go to the end with their ideas. The façade was covered with stone and the window frames replaced with a contemporary design. The structural posts were covered with metal and the old beams hidden under false ceilings. Their inspiration on the project can be appreciated on every single angle of the main room, from the sycamore veneer to the stucco wall covering. One view takes advantage of the terrace and the other of the immaculate bathroom… with the Eiffel Tower on the horizon. The living room is dominated by a large off-centre fireplace, sculptural under its fluted stone finish.

www.olivierlempereur.com

## RIGOR WITH A TOUCH OF SOFTNESS

The client was thrilled by the precision and purity of the house designed by the talented architect Marc Corbiau. His wife, however, wanted a warm interior. Thanks to Hélène and Olivier Lempereur's careful listening, her desires were fulfilled with an infusion of bright warm colours. The use of soft and welcoming materials upheld an agreement: no metal. All metal detailing were wrapped in leather. Thanks to the meticulous work of an artisan, the lava rock used for many coverings was dyed an aubergine colour. All of the furniture was designed in accordance to meticulous techniques of the great ensembliers of the 1930s. The owners got caught up in the game and asked the Lempereurs to take part in the last decorative touch of their house: selecting paintings!

www.olivierlempereur.com

# A TRIBUTE TO CONTEMPORARY ART

In this collector's apartment, art played a central role in the space planning that Hélène and Olivier elaborated. Inspiration, information and physical spaces are the ultimate key to complete the final look of the interior, art work have guided the story of the project from the beginning. For the Lempereur, heritage of work of art often determines the design of spaces: the nature and proportion of a wall, the location of a door, the light sources, and the arrangement of a room.

www.olivierlempereur.com

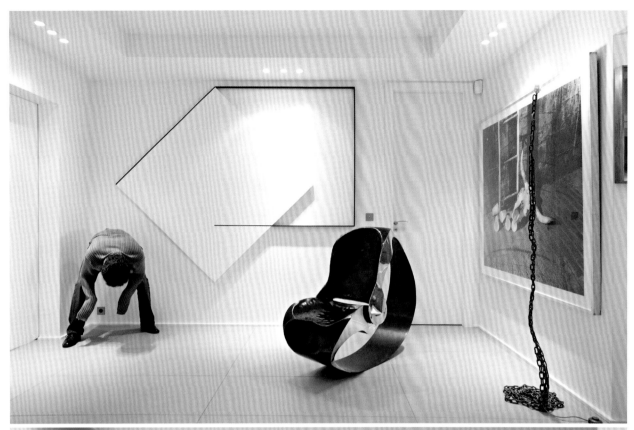

# CHIC AND COSMOPOLITAN

This is an apartment that is lived in, where people entertain, where children play and grow up. The amicable relationship that grew after a meeting with the owners enabled a subtle translation of the "couture" style embodied by the head of the household. The old parquet floor was kept as were some mouldings. On the other hand, the ceilings were reworked in keeping with the cornices in order to place mechanical elements and lighting. The furniture, perfectly designed to measure, matches rare pieces from international designers such as Ron Arad. The noblesse of the materials and the refinement of the finishing give this apartment a universal style. Its atmosphere is thoroughly cosmopolitan.

www.olivierlempereur.com

## SURROUNDED BY NATURE

This house created by the architect Bruno Erpicum is limited at the entrance side to a single level, it is weightless on the water area that separates it from the entrance avenue. To the left, the entrance shows its gallery wall. Descend a level, the construction frames the view over the fields, the countryside is yours. To the left, behind you, a series of levels interrupted by stairs that stretch outside bring the profile of the site together. To the right, beyond the overhanging part that covers the dining room, the kitchen benefits from a lateral patio that bathes in the morning sun. Go down further, the garden continues right up to the old trees in front of a swimming pool that is so long that it takes the liberty to fold back into the building through the fault-line freed up under the built-up framework.

www.alexandershouses.com

# VERTICAL WALK

The garden that separates the main part of the house is south facing, the bottom of the plot presents a level area that ends 6 metres higher up. These are the only constraints to guide the architect Bruno Erpicum, who designed a residence based on two rings: a vertical ring ensures the connection between the levels, a horizontal ring includes the earth pressure at the rear and forms the interface between the main part and the rooms on the first floor. Everything is designed so as not to have to reveal the intimacy of the premises to passers-by, in this way, only a small section of the South facing garden is reserved to welcoming visitors and the entrance to the garage. To the right, the site climbs. Steps lead you to two levels in the area bathed in light … the upper garden.

www.alexandershouses.com

## A HOUSE IN THE DUNES

This house was designed by Pieter Popeye (PVL Architects) for a retired married couple that commutes between warmer climes and the Flemish coast. It is an easy-to-maintain pied-à-terre that can be enjoyed throughout one's life, magnificently situated near dunes. The stunning views determine the dimensions, orientation and layout of the house. It is clear that the design is built from the inside out: a monumental rectangular volume in which some openings and repositionings generate interesting indoor and outdoor spaces, closed and open as necessary.

www.pvlarchitecten.be

↖
The contrasting use of
materials on this level
(wenge parquet floors,
white Carrara marble
for countertops and
wall cladding and white
lacquered cabinet work)
creates a perfect harmony:
warm, yet with a strong
feeling of space.

# PEACE AND QUIET

This haven of peace and quiet was created near Kortrijk and nestles in a green oasis. The existing house was completely redesigned by interior architect Steven Compernol in collaboration with architect Rudy Vandeputte. The synergy between interior and exterior was the starting point for this conversion. Both the design and materials used are the result of this interaction. The result is a interplay of closed volumes with surprising openings and views to the garden all around.

www.space-design.be      www.archi2.be

The kitchen appears to have been cut from the wooden wall that runs throughout the ground floor. Stainless steel contrasts with the warm wood and rough stone wall.

The relaxing area occupies the entire front side. Study, fitness and games room follow each other with the theme being the wall of books that connects these spaces.

↖
The various successive areas can be fully opened up to create a single large living space. The uninterrupted wooden wall reinforces this sense of space. The suspended ceiling provides a high level of acoustic comfort.

## A REAL METAMORPHOSIS

A new wing was added to the existing L-shaped house, built around the existing sunken terrace.
It was conceived as a glass box, partly with windows, partly white enamelled glass.
The challenge was to create a canopy that would only be 15mm thick. A sunken
swimming pool with its own terraces was built in line with the new wing.
The existing buildings were completely refurbished. A first floor was added
over part of the original building with a roof clad in copper.
Also the entire interior design of the building was done by the Aurora-projects
company, in line with the plans created by the architect Pascal van der Kelen.

www.pascalvanderkelen.com    www.aurora-interiors.com

View of the completely renovated dining room. The windows were shifted out as a continuous wall. This reinforces the contrast between the old framework and the new structures. A second fireplace was designed for the dining room.

Views of the new wing. The space has been designed to offer extra height, so that the very large works of art can be displayed here. "Bench" in pin oak with boiled wool upholstery. "Coffee Table" in lacquered structure and white epoxy resin. Both from the pascalvanderkelencollection, manufactured by www.aurora-interiors.com. To the left of the fireplace, the architect realized a niche with zenithal light to highlight the beautiful sculpture by Juan Munoz.
Other works of art by Franz West (in the garden), Gunther Forge, Yves Klein and Panamarenko.

↖
View from the library to the new wing with the living area.
Works of art by Kenneth Noland, Imi Knoebel and Franz West.

# A HOLIDAY FEELING IN A CONTEMPORARY SETTING

The principals, both very active people in their 40s with a busy agenda, wanted to convert the villa they had bought and which lies in thickly wooded surroundings into a place where coming home means living in another world, in which there is room for professional and domestic activities and in which a holiday feeling can never be far away either. There was also a request to maximise the contact with the garden and to build a covered, outdoor space in the garden. The building was completely stripped. The heavy outdoor woodwork was replaced by something more elegant in aluminium and new window openings were also provided at several precisely selected places. Indoor walls were removed or added here and there, for the sake of programme requirements or for architectural reasons. This purified and strengthened the qualities of the original rooms.

www.steinvanrossem.be

Custom built kitchen with a view of the fixed cupboard wall and the cooking area and baking oven placed centrally.

Entry zone with a free-standing couch and incorporated hand washer. Various panels in the wooden walls of black tinted oak act as doors.

↖
Living area with the fireplace and the custom built coffee table in black tinted oak. In analogy to the indoor area, a fireplace has also been installed outdoors.

# WHERE ART MEETS ARCHITECTURE

Older homes have a right to a new life, both in terms of building physics and aesthetically.
The private home of Ar+ architecture and interior projects is a good example of this.
Durable quality and attention to detail, purity, light and soberness are central.
The result: an impressive transformation with a strong passion for art.

www.arplus.be

The library contains books about artists from the world of art, architecture, photography and music. The long, narrow band window at the bottom offers a view of the water, but if there is a need for privacy on the street side, it can be covered by a sliding panel. Large work of art by Arie de Groot.

In the dining area, a round dining table with marble top by Eero Saarinen. Chairs by Charles and Ray Eames. Ceiling-height, frameless inner doors with delicate white door handles almost disappear into the wall.

↖
The monumental entrance hall highlights the contrast between the existing low ceilings and the new high ceilings that reflect the gallery feeling of a museum. Large floor tiles of sandblasted Carrara marble and a recessed coconut mat at the entrance door. A one-seater by Le Corbusier. Works of art by the German Barbara Koch and the Austrian Eva Schlegel.

The existing low ceilings automatically create zones for different functions such as lounge and dining area. Open spaces and roof lights were part of the design thirty years ago, and still provide a feeling of transparency and spaciousness. Artworks by Renaat Ivens and Willy De Sauter. Sofa: Piero Lissoni by Cassina.

## A WHITE AND SUNNY HIDEAWAY

Above all else, the builders wanted an abundance of light and a house which gave them that real holiday feeling all year round. With this in mind, the architect, Baudouin Courtens, devised a house of pure lines, a series of white spaces positioned in amongst the greenery. A house which he then opened up to the sun by choosing and carefully framing views of the garden. The concept is pushed to its limits: the floors, walls and ceilings on the ground floor are all white, the windows allow nature scenes to burst into the house like living paintings, immersing the inhabitants in the poetry of the passing seasons.

www.courtens.be

# THE LUXURY OF SPACE

Space is a luxury…
…and in this magnificent creation by Marc Corbiau, the spaces are nothing short of majestic.
Ensemble & Associés have recreated the fittings, finishes and atmosphere of this
home in order to best meet the requirements of its new owners. Simple materials and
colours, flowing lines and efficient organisation are all hallmarks of the design.

www.ensembleetassocies.be

Bookcase and desk, custom-made in white painted MDF.

↖
White leather Edra
settees and grey velvet
Edra armchair.
Low oval table designed
by Ensemble & Associés
with black stone top.
Saint-Laurent, base and top
made of polished chrome.
Rug by Bic Carpets.

# A PASSION FOR CONTEMPORARY ART

In a house whose lines were decided by architect Bruno Moinard (an interior designer from Paris), Obumex architect Vangroenweghe has achieved a fitting interior. The interior had to be the perfect background for the owner's artworks. So Obumex applied his proven, timeless trademarks and experience to this top project.

www.obumex.be

A floor in Bianco Statuario and artworks by Rosita Fernandez and Tivi.

Table, chairs and couches by Christian Liaigre in white leather. A dark blue carpet by Treutlin. The lacework truck is by the Belgian artist Wim Delvoye. The blue screen work is by Heimo Zobernig.

↖
The floor consists of oak planks selected by Obumex.
Blue seats by B&B Italia and a one-seater in salmon-coloured leather by Promemoria. The coffee tables are an artwork by Yves Klein. The gymnast is a work by Opi. The fireplace wall was custom made by Obumex.

A white Augustin
seat and a table with
gold by Klein.

# A UNIQUE AND PERSONAL COMBINATION

Damien Langlois-Meurinne is a designer and interior architect based in Paris. He worked for Christian Liaigre and received a commission from Zimmer + Rohde to design his first line of furniture, before going on to create his own studio, Agence dl-m, which works on a wide variety of projects: offices and showrooms, and also private homes. In every project, the objective is not to impose a specific style, but to create an interior that is completely in harmony with the location and the client. For Damien Langlois-Meurinne, each project is a very personal combination of a number of elements, including the place, the owner, the function and the budget. He always pays close attention to these elements to create appropriate and elegant design.

www.dl-m.fr

The floor, wall and kitchen work surface are in lava stone.
The table, with its Corian surface and sculpted granite feet, is by
dl-m. Hanging lamp in brass with a bronze finish.

Bath in a Juneda natural stone. Dornbracht taps. Bronze door
handles.

↖
A white gloss shelving unit with sycamore boxes
that can be illuminated in different colours.
An old oak parquet.
The wool sofas with steel feet and the coffee
tables in glossy walnut wood are designs
by Damien Langlois-Meurinne.
A partition wall made of tinted oak panels.
A hand-made carpet from Tibet.
The chair in solid tinted oak is a creation by Agence dl-m.

# A FASCINATING CONFRONTATION

Architect Pascal van der Kelen has created a fascinating confrontation between contemporary art, design and architecture in this beautiful townhouse.

www.pascalvanderkelen.com

# AN EXCEPTIONAL ART COLLECTION
# IN A CONTEMPORARY CASTLE

In a completely restored castle, gallery Guy Pieters selected a collection of exception works of contemporary art: Gilbert & George, Andy Warhol,...

www.modern-art-foundation.com

# MASTERWORKS

In a timeless country house, gallery Guy Pieters chose some
masterworks of contemporary artists: Pierre Alechinsky,
Robert Indiana, Lucio Fontana, Andy Warhol,...

www.modern-art-foundation.com

## A SPLENDID BLEND

The late Sophie Campion has created the interior of this spacious house near Brussels: a splendid blend of antiques, contemporary art and timeless design.

# AN APARTMENT IN BEJING

This apartment is located in East Beijing, adjacent to the Kunlun Hotel.
The apartment building has two towers with full-floor glass curtains.
Seven model rooms were created for the East Tower with
a total construction area of about 360m².
This apartment, designed by Lee Wei Min (LWM Architects), has
three bedrooms (one room for a study) and two halls.

www.lwma.com

Each bedroom has its own independent use of the bathroom; the whole is equipped with intelligent control systems and a lighting sensor system with automatic curtain blinds and a fresh air system.

# INSPIRED BY LE CORBUSIER

The design of this duplex apartment designed by Albert Ho and Jensu Hou was inspired by Le Corbusier's color study in general and his Femmes XX$^e$ siècle, 1935 in particular. The clients requested that the design be modern without minimalist white and cold grey - the apartment was to welcome their eleven-month-old twins. In recalling how wonderful light and color transformed the interiors of Le Corbusier's 'white boxes', the designers asked the client to embark on an adventure in color. After a series of studies, Hu & Hou settled on a color scheme of four primary colours: maroon, light olive green and a light and dark shade of beige. These became the most important guide in organizing plane elements and volumes. They helped define the flow of spaces from one area or floor to the next as well as spatial boundaries within each room.

www.hohou.com

The main stairway is clad in stained oak while the solid rail has a textured maroon Formica panel. The flooring materials consist of beige travertine tiles, olive-green linoleum, and maroon-coloured concrete. And finally, the ceilings read like a series of horizontal color canvasses.

# TSAI'S RESIDENCE, TAIPEI

This project designed by Schichieh Lu is a combination of
two units on Dunhua South Road in Taipei.
Based on the owner's request, the entire space was re-divided into two sections:
the "master bedroom section" for everyday living and the "guestroom section"
for parents who visit the owner occasionally.

Living room and dining room are combined to form a bigger space.
The kitchen is like an island in an open space. The multidimensional stone-cut and diamond-cut counter top of the kitchen set creates the sense of an artificial stone island. Furniture decorates the space and balances the pure style of the original space and brings out the taste for life of the designer and owners.

A huge glass wall between the living room and the bedroom maintains the continuation of two spaces. Curtains are the main elements used to separate the rooms.

# A PERFECT BALANCE

This four-story house (650 m² in total) is part of the Yongtai Xianshang residential project located in Haidian District, north-west of Beijing city. The unique L construction applied to the architectural design for the outside is used to create as much privacy as possible. The design makes full use of its minimalist and practical characteristics by dropping any unnecessary complications in spatial division. In this way residents can utilize the space according to their individual needs, arranging it freely. Yongtai Xianshang residence combines contemporary designs with human living concerns, achieving a balance between aesthetics and practicality.

www.mwa.com.tw

# A FRESH PERSPECTIVE

There will probably be many operations of this type in the areas surrounding our towns in the future. Land which is not built on will become rare and property as a whole will need to be significantly renovated. The "Dandoy" house was built in the 1960s at the request of a doctor. The house reveals a complicated layout, has little light, contains obsolete fittings and was built using techniques which are no longer used and the insulation is not perfect either. The new occupant requested that the architect approached the building with a completely fresh perspective with a view to creating a modern and comfortable home.

www.erpicum.org

Black leather for the Le Corbusier cubes. Extra colour from the window looking out onto the garden.

Kitchen created by Poggenpohl.

# LES HEURES CLAIRES

The work involves renovating and transforming a house in the suburbs into a contemporary residential building. The owner wanted everything to have a fresh perspective, to be rethought and reworked: The architect took charge of the building and worked on it as if it were a sculpture which needs to be controlled from both the inside and the outside until a full appreciation is gained for the relationship the occupants have with the building in question. The architect will work on the house relentlessly, applying his formula of preference: "the right proportions shall have precedence over any form of decoration". Since, two white walls have appeared on the avenue in the suburbs and two young trees can be seen in front of these walls which will grow and bear witness to the seasons of the year.

www.erpicum.org

The lounge is extended by multimedia living room located in the old section of the house.

The "John Pawson Kitchen System" has been created by Obumex.

# A LIVING BOX

A box built for living purposes and given its home within the forest. Raised just a few centimetres from the earth, it appears as if the building makes every effort not to disturb the tranquillity of the site. Inside, the rooms are surrounded by a glass curtain which weaves through the box without ever touching the external walls of the structure. The curtain is used instead of blank walls and incorporates two patios which separate the bedrooms from the living rooms. Much in the style of colonial residential buildings, the building has an ambulatory around the outside where residents can enjoy a stroll and also benefit from being in the shade. A project by architect Bruno Erpicum.

www.erpicum.org

The furniture has been selected by the designer Bruno Reymond - La Maison de l'Eléphant store – and compliments the monochrome appearance of the building.

## BEAUTIFUL VIEWS

The house is laid out across two plateaux. From the upper plateau, which was previously the site of a riding school, we can see that the countryside stretches right to the village. Three separate buildings are located on the upper plateau which house the garage and bedrooms. The buildings are all accessible via a dual walkway along which screen walls are dotted which frame the views from the property and provide privacy for the respective patios. There is a forest on the other side. The rooms used for living purposes are located in an extremely large building, the height of which increases as the land descends towards the lower plateau. A vast bay window to the left reveals the surrounding landscape whilst the surface of the water located to the right on a lower level reflects the sky and the forest. The living room also has a stone terrace which goes as far as the swimming pool. From there, the view overlooks the countryside and the sea and the horizon beyond.

www.erpicum.org

220

The furniture in the house is by designer Bruno Reymond – from la Maison de l'Eléphant store –.

# A DESIGNER'S HOME IN CAPE TOWN

Project architects Richard Townsend and Stefan Antoni used a 'sea-farm' inspiration to create
a holiday house for a small family in Cape Town (South Africa). The house was to have
a feature double volume space with very simple clean lines and needed to flow seamlessly
between interior and exterior. The clients, being in the design world, were particularly sensitive
to colour and were very much involved in choosing the materials used in both the interior
and exterior of the home. The interior decor was designed by Beth Murray who was involved
with both the architects and the clients from an early stage in the project.  What began as a
holiday home for a bachelor is now a permanent residence for a small family.   The design
is far more sensitive than the vernacular concrete and glass look of the surrounding area.
It is more African and contextual, yet still manages to retain it's originally intended holiday feel.

www.saota.com

The view from the deck towards the entrance of the house showing the glass balustrade bridge and stairway.

The glass balustraded bridge with timber flooring, leads to the more private bedroom areas upstairs.

↖
A floating kitchen unit, designed by Stefan Antoni, is made in a walnut finish. Stainless steel, glass and black granite finishes complement the open plan dining area which reinforces the holiday feel of the home in its simplicity and style. The dining furniture is also designed by Stefan Antoni and made in oak and walnut.

## OPEN YET PRIVATE

The clients requested a sculptured building with clean horizontal lines, large areas of glass and screens creating a space 'open as well as private'. The Cove, a Private Estate in South Africa, with the Pezula Golf Estate as backdrop. The site, located on an exposed cliff edge overlooking a rocky peninsula is perched above a dramatic seascape with spectacular views. Its owner's wanted a house with seamless indoor-outdoor living for summer holiday retreats. The house has to take maximum advantage of the spectacular views and surrounding landscape. The site falls within a pristine and unique environment that required a careful understanding of the natural attributes of the site.

www.saota.com

## INTIMATE AND COSY

A project by Simone Kengo in a 250m² apartment in Walloon Brabant, with furniture from her interior-design company Minimal Interior: two 1932 Dossier droit poufs in greige leather by Jean-Michel Frank (Ecart International), a Lounge sofa and two Normandie armchairs with detachable covers by Catherine Memmi, and a Chelsea coffee table, also by Catherine Memmi. Painting by Pierre Debatty; carpet by Bartholomeus.

minimalinterior@skynet.be

All of the furniture in this dining room by Simone Kengo (Minimal Interior) was designed by Catherine Memmi. Carpet by Bartholomeus.

Contrasting colours and materials in this design by Simone Kengo (Minimal Interior).
Chest of drawers with leather handles and bed frame, both in oak with mocha satin finish (Catherine Memmi). Bedcover in taupe velvet. Linen carpet by Bartholomeus.

## DOWN TO BASICS

This office is in a new building " Koninklijk Entrepôt " by the well-known
German architect Kollhoff in the trendy Eilandje district of Antwerp.
The studio of Cy Peys interior architects was able to get down to basics: existing walls
were demolished in order to redefine the spaces according to the wishes of the client.
The design aims to create a contrast between the different spaces: a dark entrance
hall, warm colours in the director's office and a white space for the secretary.

www.cypeys.com

The simply designed kitchen is beside the director's office. Tall bar stools for informal dining and for meetings.

PUBLISHER
BETA-PLUS publishing
www.betaplus.com

PHOTOGRAPHY
Jo Pauwels

DESIGN
Polydem – Nathalie Binart

ISBN : 978-90-8944-114-0

Coordination production printing and binding :
www.belvedere.nl - André Kloppenberg
Printing and binding:  Printer Trento, Italy

# LONGWOOD PUBLIC LIBRARY
**800 Middle Country Road**
**Middle Island, NY 11953**
**(631) 924-6400**
**mylpl.net**

## LIBRARY HOURS

| | |
|---|---|
| Monday-Friday | 9:30 a.m. - 9:00 p.m. |
| Saturday | 9:30 a.m. - 5:00 p.m. |
| Sunday (Sept-June) | 1:00 p.m. - 5:00 p.m. |